SHEARSMAN

101 & 102

WINTER 2014 / 2015

EDITOR
TONY FRAZER

Shearsman magazine is published in the United Kingdom by
Shearsman Books Ltd
50 Westons Hill Drive | Emersons Green | BRISTOL BS16 7DF

Editor: Tony Frazer

Registered office: 30-31 St James Place, Mangotsfield, Bristol BS16 9JB
(this address not for correspondence)
www. shearsman.com
ISBN 978-1-84861-383-6
ISSN 0260-8049

Subscriptions and single copies

Current subscriptions—covering two double-issues, with an average length of
108 pages—cost £14 for delivery to U.K. addresses, £17 for the rest of Europe
(including the Republic of Ireland), and £19 for the rest of the world. Longer
subscriptions may be had for a pro-rata higher payment. North American
customers will find that buying single copies from online retailers in the U.S.A. will
be cheaper than subscribing. £19 equated to more than $31 at the time we went
to press, and single copies cost $14 at full-price retail in the U.S.A. The reason for
this discrepancy is that overseas postage rates in the U.K. have been rising rapidly,
whereas copies of the magazine are also printed in the U.S.A. to meet local demand
from online retailers there, and thus avoid the transatlantic journey.

Back issues from n° 63 onwards (uniform with this issue)—cost £8.50 / $14
through retail outlets. Single copies can be ordered for £8.50, post-free, direct from
the press, through the Shearsman Books online store, or from bookstores in the U.K.
and the U.S.A. Issues of the old pamphlet-style version of the magazine, from
n° 1 to 62, may be had for £3 each, direct from the press, where they are still
available, but contact us for a quote for a full, or partial, run.

Submissions

Shearsman operates a submissions-window system, whereby submissions are only
accepted during the months of March and September, when selections are
made for the October and April issues, respectively. Submissions may be sent
by mail or email, but email attachments—other than PDFs—are not accepted.
We aim to respond within 3 months of the window's closure.

Acknowledgement

María do Cebreiro's poem 'Loyalty', in Neil Anderson's translation,
previously appeared in the online magazine *M-Dash*.

Contents

Nathan Shepherdson

the trawler

for Alun Leach-Jones

a common parliament of seagulls
ensures a consistent level of demand and abuse
as the catch hits the trawler deck
fresh human heads flopping around in panic
bright colours amass as pointillist glints
some scales around the eyes so gold
you'd swear they were bounty
off skeletous hands unshaken for centuries

the gills a recent evolutionary curiosity
composed slits starting behind the ear
and following the line of the jaw
now out of water
flare with asthmatic inefficiency

the tails an eonic transformation of hair
a glutinous muscle keratin coat
tapered with eel ingenuity from back of scalp
now physically protest their depleted energy
to indifferent splinters on the killing floor
aware that in non-liquid space
function might as well be a wreath

we need to remind our fishmonger selves
that there is no profit in admiration
and if all echoes are removed from any scenario
we will hear what we are supposed to hear
that hard work is the best Christian answer

the first heads we throw back are the politicians
opposite to romantic suicides but just as poisonous

celebrity heads look good but are tasteless
scientific heads taste great but might kill you
the heads of our own families are out of the question
and military heads might explode on the first bite
musical heads are fine but can repeat on you
the heads of poets though reputedly excellent to eat
are alas tossed away because of low market value
the prize heads are philosophers and artists
the filleted cheeks a noted delicacy
the white flesh lean and stained with mistakes
it flakes like fondant savoury talc
a thread from the tongue to St Peter's table

§

for 25 years you've lived in a tank on my desk
and despite habitat taunts to both of us
you remain happy
not just because i spared your life
but because our intellect locks two elements
and dispenses molecules as a means of affection
and when i need to clean your water
i briefly hold you in my hands
and still marvel how each scale is a mirror
in this interlaced blue wrinkle-free foil
even thoughts are reflected
in the fact that i've never seen another since
the world fell into the ocean
and you returned to the surface
knowing the human line of thousands of rewound lives

i've had many offers from emporia
their saliva behind dam walls made of knives
their washed plates as ready as sin
but there is no temptation
because my impotence in all this
creates your strength to exist
your blood colder than mine and more perfect
age has refused to tie you to any clock

and one day my bones will become ornaments
on the gravel beneath your fins

if anything
we allow a skerrick of authentic fantasy
'a skerrick'- in such a word
the second r can be turned backwards
to form a bridge
with a small but unbreachable gap
where we suspend and are suspended in each other's minds

but for now all we can do
is imagine our different paths to oxygen
while i continue to feed you krill and commas
our gourami glass kiss
as important as the glazier's phone number

silver
   for Tom Shapcott

the two whole notes

deep in the ears of John the Bapist
fell just short of holding enough musical energy
to open his eyes one last time

this would've been a miracle
for a head on a platter

one speaker without wires

seismographic innuendo
charts the new shore around his neck

ragged veins
in complete conversation with silver

how sleep designs a mirror

walking through stone
and into measurement
i cut my colour
from the sun

tuning another hand
to the same splinter
is how ambition
attracts the company
of rust ←

what is this order of bones
restacked in a pyramid
every 24 hours
in lipless ritual
on a bed
that dreams of sleep
is why i'm here
patting the stoic dog
that has been trained
to carry my skull
to the end
of my first sentence

now it's the floor
that walks towards me
on unnamed bones
the calcium ground
into flour to rise in bread
baked in the metal scale model
of an apostle's lung

i denounce hunger to feed light

replace the fluid in the veins
with no fluid in the veins

to think absence into solid form
perhaps a cube
that yesterday was sand
and today is covered in bark
waiting to shed itself
somewhere in an autoqueue of insects
patrolling the smallest stains
left by a wounded nightmare
that has every chance
but no hope
of waking up

the fool climbs the mountain
to view what wise men forget →
paints a landscape in intricate detail
with a brush crafted from hair
from his own eyebrows
when complete
paints over it entire in white
only to paint over it again in black
then return with his picture
to sell it to his shadow
at a cold price determined
by the accuracy of memory

as a target
i make love
to the vantage point
of the arrow
not the arrow itself (→)
blind enough
to smell the space
buffering a plain cross
on a forehead light years away
as close as the fingertips
of the archer's cocked hand

no doubt
this is someone ←
who ably presents himself
at the unmanned counter
in this library of violence
who seeks to withdraw
the necessity of the act
but not the act itself
ably inscribed
with the same nail
as a fate of individual numbers
prominent on leathered organs
captive in vinegar
in jars that do not end a line
which one day will tilt
and draw itself back
towards the eye
as it ignites a vigil of burning tongues
that give off words instead of smoke
either side of the second sky
traded entire for the first seed
planted dark into new silence

(0)

i am the animals limping to the blood dairy

i am the gold i inject into every iris

i am the key inserted in the earth

↕

you carve the night
into a somersault
and pray you end up
under its feet

Cristina Viti

from At Fifty

II

a painfully delicious sharpening of taste
dawn-red, lysergic, irredeemably altered
blunt it you die streaming curses

or wind up crawling at the oracle hole

who are you then worshipper
devoid of all purity
your goddess detritus clogging the gut of the word

who are you bliss whore
forehead splitting like a dead fruit on marble steps
fingers twitching a nightmare of statues' smiles

you are the scroll written & rewritten
with all the pain of the many worlds
a palimpsest of bruises in the guano of cathedral spires

until you learn to sing your mind's eye
into breathing the world alive

or else it's down

languages a haircloth belt at the waste of language
stabbed brain of no way in or out
raw-picked scab of habit

down

butchered heart of powerless devotion
poleaxed backbone of injured sovereignty
red raw apron of afterbirthed straight talk

amor vacui: to be fire, devour devour devour

as women cross town with their useless gift-wrapped hearts
        their spines are broken accordions badly stacked card decks
                            waterlogged filing cabinets

    their spines are cracked masts weeping cancers of amber

black mothers undone by love calcinate in the sun
                as roomfuls of old mija nuncles
                        wait for a nod from the head boy

but out here there are breezes my love
        wild enough to land profligate blizzards of cherry blossom
            into the womb of a man & watch him birth

    whole new orchards of bright words

            & there are scents in the words' folds sometimes

turn me into an old painter man & I will bend you to me
        for the cruelty of creation knows no bounds
            I will bend you to me in a game of noughts & crosses

you nought me your cross the heart of an old painter
                        is a garment of white sugar

for the joy of creation knows no bounds
        my scrotum an egg sac of eyes I take out
                    & throw at the plumbline of the sun

as ideograms melt & slide down your skin

            your kidneys will sing like wagtails as you learn
                to dance by bitch-licking me on a speeding train

& if I beg you in private mock you in public have mercy
        for my starkness requires your body that knows

how to turn from a sliver of ice
    to a well-leavened loaf to a leashed labrador & then back again
        in the time that it takes a lovebite to fade

O requiem aeternam pretty mama
    sweet Catholic wench
        with your kundalini crown to fight

you too must make way with your storms & your curses

    & I will come home a gentle flower
      a dead green stick with a head
        exploding in silent elegies of colour

    what better way to live or to die

except that at fifty if I listen my voice is breaking like that
    of a fifteen-year-old boy & like a fifteen-year-old boy
        I grow skittish & haggard & easily bored

is there any any is there nonesuch
    poem as will call herself by name & surname
      & stop hiding in the folds of the cloak of some wounded
                    [mythical queen

O poetry come quick
    lay your hand between my hipbones that I may remember
        this my fifty-year old matrix as now it is

a smooth-spinning radar
    a globe of soft white light
      a slow dynamo of tenderness

    their theories at the ready like brittle pencils
      but some souls have as many ages as many sexes
              as a waterfall

*

daily work like a bone needle & big
    cross stitches of red thread a seal
        skin door for the heart's iglu

skin goes & then muscle & then blood
    roses layered in the ice mirror of the singing skull

fractured heart vertebra
    almond tree by the swamp
        dark house of my voice

        witch-doctor soft chuckle
          you want sexual healing ha –
            that's the easy bit jimmybones

you who come with red wine like death's lipstick
    expecting to dine at creatively unpredictable times
        on my shadow that's orange & blue

        but turns Aztec verdigris & it burns you

as the dead pull me softly by the hair
    past pillars of undersea song
        any wonder at fifty I'll pray

so help me god if I'm to lose all grace & all velocity
        then turn me god
    you Andalusian dog of all torment then turn me

into a haystack of hairless tongues
    a wineskin of washerwoman wit
        a flinty wisp of sharp a fishwife's hook

don't cry baby don't cry look here see

already I have sent the festal red skirt to the gospodina
       & you shall marry with solstice bells at noon

already I have mixed the kind nepenthe
       & you'll have no memory of strange days like these

when we lay together
       like the two lips of a wound closing

or when
       in a filthy bed
              we fucked life clean

*

Fie, fie, Cecilia! Your sweet Italian music......

Ray DiPalma

Princely Sport

No restrictions none
As privileged as fugal
Close to the hurt of things
Misheard, judged so only
To surprise you when you
Most expect it—the fugue
After all—coming and going
But back before you know it,
Though you did all along—
The briefness of expectation,
Myshkin, kept you tongue-tied
Nothing else to be added and
In need of no further conviction
There the moment of privilege

The Evaluative As Invocation

Red on white
Red rather than white
Distinctly opposed
While whispered in capture
Whispered against
In an intrigue of the chastened
The chastened by the unheard
Red warped out of white
Red amused by white
Endless conjoined finalities
Respective incipit in refraction
Circumscribed by variance
And such the such
The perseverant horlieu of minima

From a Skeptic's Notebook:
A White Paper on the Blue Plate Special

Incapable of waiting
the sirens follow the course
of an illogical pattern of events
fully sanctioned but
not yet safely concluded

A five hour siege
while waiting to order—
and no asylum on the end of the fork
—anonymous and anyhow
the mechanisms

Perfumed x-rays dusty cluttered and black
skull the menu
A sign on the jukebox reads
TO BE RESOLVED MUSICALLY ELSEWHERE
Simmered covered

Troika

            Nothing alien to its self-accord—

Too far off
time exists
by exclusion
as does what
is mine only
by division—
that much less
become so much more
by this conversion.

Sunlight loosens
only what wanted
to be—not what
wanted to be here.
A huddle of
risk potential
or lack of discretion?

Brought like song
only to say, not
to teach, always
held in belief
by some few,
always beyond
pace and disclosure.

Saturday Avatar

Aroused and clicking
In the darkened room

Any likeness a perfect fit
Objects of balance in all its forms

Caesura of pestilence
Creaking in the wind

A slot for a mouth
Takes up where the oracle left off

Deciduous pluck then metamorphosis
All on the same page

Mark Goodwin

Something Slips Through Lock Gates at Foxton

noise like wind through
a complex of twigs

as notes are blown off

-key   through the

crack by the hinge
white froth rotates

a lock-keeper's accordion's
white keys tremble as

the black ones thump

algaed blue-bricks are
loaves of a gone

-world's bread

listen   a metal smell of sluiced
utterances about ocean

water's noise creased
between lock jaws

a sky being wound to rope

the lock-keeper's fingers curl
round his lock-key's startling iron
as frost's revolution inlays

scrolls along a long black hull

each lock's mechanism holds
repeated glugs & crick

-cracks of past's silence

the judder of a paddle
travelling its ratchet is
every boat that's

ever passed here all

hulls water's held

the lock keeper's brow seeps
salty silvery threads as August
sun cooks ditch-stink   each

peninsula of
lock-lever boasts

a lit tip a

water-white light
house on
a black head
land poking

out in

to a sea of
green mid
land hillside

peninsulas repeated as
steps up through

a house of water or
a house of hill

a lock-keeper's pressed
wet glistening bones stretch
from hill

bottom to hill

     top

his whole elastic
    skeleton is rills &

roars &
    trickles &

     hollow

passionate glugs from
hill top to hill

     bottom

each paddle winding-post has
a toothed bar like a child's

vertebral column

dark grease glistens
on the column's metal notches

on cool mornings dew
collects on the grease

air delivers some

thing a lock-keeper's wri

ggling accordion
is a cage of cla
cking ribs or

fingers of white
aerated water &
black lock-levers of

flats & sharps   his

wife's voice hides
in the faint hiss
of spray

gathering on grass as a

lock-keeper plays

like minerals dissolving
in water or water's

patient evaporation   his

music is
a cold

wet flare yet
dry as by a

hundred years
of fireside

Electric

my boy & I swim
in my dad's lake

today the lake is crinkled slate
a liquid rattling of dark
corrugation pressed

by a bulbous evolving sky

                                    thunder's sub

stance inflates space & colours and

       yet

its vast hollow thuds prick pin

-point sharp where

                        we are

my boy's eyes spark
with controlled terror

and free amazement

back-dropped by
pumped-up purple
the tall willows are
metallic-green and vibrate as

air begins and

         ends on

each fish-shaped leaf

wind peels off
    faint but crisp
        layers of light
            grey lake-spray

my boy & I hang
in undulating water   we
scrunch our eyes as

        suddenly hail

pixelates our faces
the lake's pocked wrig

            gling skin sizzles

my boy's rapturous voice blurs
with a world's ringing
layers and my

        voice joins his

a dripping crow hunkers
in the lantern of the young
sycamore by the stile

a startled moorhen drags
her fast trail of watery arrows
into the reeds' *shrish*

shelter for our bodies
is a whole house

    of lake

my boy & I are two heads
poked into air's storm bobbing
on a trembling membrane as

        our bodies hang

23

swayed in the lake's first
moments of depth quiet

below us where

      fish wait in soft silts

                above us

sky's miles rise
through electric clouds

suddenly light

        ening takes

all space away and in
stantly gives

      back all time as

           A

        single place

              etched-in-flash

my boy & I laugh and

        laugh a life

      time's

          glee-&-fright

Lucy Sheerman

from Fragments Salvaged From Her Diary:
A Correspondence with *Rebecca*

XI

A pause, a moment of agony. The visit has lasted long enough.
Everything is charming. The room revolving on its axis, around
the arm chair and the carriage clock. Another ghost skimming
these surfaces. I rise clumsily from the table, shaking the cups and
saucers. 'I want to glide across these rooms once again', says the
thin querulous voice. 'To be swept up. Away.' She has lost the gift,
of being charmed. I reach for her fingertips, hoping to touch. It is
futile. Escaping into silence. It is all a blur. I have lost colour. My face
fades in every mirror. Exposed to sunlight. My skin is too thin, my
lips brittle. 'I don't mind, I don't mind'.

XII

They are straining against this pale ghost now. My childish wandering
always leading them away. I wonder: why should Maxim dislike her
cousin? The longing to take that other path. Those hot blue eyes,
that loose mouth and the careless familiar laugh. Imagine looking
from these windows with those eyes and in different shoes. Trying
things on for size. It was wrong, out of all proportion. They were all
watching and laughing. Defending him. Resenting every footstep,
waiting for every false step. A slight awkwardness whenever his
name was mentioned. Patience for the slow turning back. Another
dead end. I must retrace her steps to the beginning. Sitting where
she sat now. At each end of a long table. Separated and formal.
As I watched, she would get up from her chair with a quick glance
at him. Reminded of that very first sight of her, up on the cliff.
She would begin talking about something different. The sickening
vertigo. Love swooping her upwards. My own dull self did not exist.
Seen through adult eyes, 'You look like a little criminal, what is it?'
He cannot see what they can.

XIII

Identical. The same picture, the same dress. Light and laughter fill-
ing the rooms, drifting against the hems of this terrible outfit, and the
music. Hearing the hollow sound of my footsteps on the stairs. I did
not dance. I went on staring at the empty chairs. I was transformed.
The costume folded away, the pristine slippers. I unwound the little
story I had spun. He did not belong to me at all. Over, long before
midnight. He did not try and stop me. Upstaged, I looked up and
saw I was myself again. Here to watch him speak his lines at the
dress rehearsal. She was haunting me through him. He would never
love me. Play acting, I was forgetting my cue. They asked me the
same questions as if I might eventually recall what to say. Perfectly
marvellous. I was caught in the blaze of attention. Who was I to
stand at his side, suffering with stage fright. She was still mistress of
Manderley. She was still Mrs de Winter.

XIV

Where is she? What have you done with her? Air heavy like water; like
a slow poison. Her, always her. Flesh has melted. I cannot lie still.
Wherever I walk, wherever I sit, in my thoughts and in my dreams,
I meet her. The ache that will not ease no matter how I lie. Almost
touching. Hands that wrote 'Max from *Rebecca*' on the fly leaf of
a book. A noise, as if from far away. Among a thousand others, I
should recognise her voice. I shall never be rid of her. Darkness
receding into the blue. Heartless. Sightless. Heavier than air. Pressed
down on the coverlet. Light seeping onto my fingertips. A kind of
warmth I suppose. She would never grow old. I could not fight. She
was too strong. Perhaps I'd forgotten how it felt. This freedom from
consequence. As I said her name it sounded strange and sour like a
forbidden word, a relief to me no longer, hot and shaming as a sin
confessed. Delirious. Eyes black. He doesn't love me. Desire weigh-
ing me down. I would kill her all over again. I feel the slow burning
across my skin. I hear him give a startled cry but I do not care.

XV

A living breathing woman like myself, flesh and blood. I knew she was waiting. It was only a matter of time. I turned the handle of the door and went inside. The hating had fixed onto me. Keeping her vividly alive. Go on, don't be afraid. I shut my eyes. This exquisite pain was a dull reflection of the real hurt. Soon I would not have to think about her any more... I was disappearing. Dissolved. It was the stillness of the black water, the unknown things that lay beneath. Far away beneath the surface. Keeping us apart. Why can't we start again? The risk of repeating ourselves. Falling into the same trap. I stared at him, my hands cold beneath his. Surprised into feeling. We are undisturbed. No, you don't understand. Exposed. Trembling. I knelt watching his face, watching his eyes. I could not speak. Pulling away. 'No,' I said. 'No'. Pushing against him. It is the body of some unknown woman, unclaimed, belonging nowhere. Claiming the longing. Here was an answer. The ache that pierced me for so long had gone. She was not drowned at all. Heat and fierce kisses on cool skin. I am liquid. Holding my breath. 'I carried her body to the cabin, and took the boat out that night and sunk it there'. I look away. I am forsaking all others. 'Will you look into my eyes and tell me that you love me now?' And suddenly I have my moment. We have arrived together at the same point. Just in time.

XVI

Over and over, there's that same refrain, taking me back through these moments, swaying. A dance, each step a perfect match. I stare at him stupidly. Forward and back. The awkward turns twisting us together and apart. Holding me so close I can feel his heart beat. He had killed her. She had not been drowned at all. They might have suspected, they might have guessed. I see it now. The way he never mentioned her name. Holding on for dear life. Not to have him now would be to die. Touching but not seeing, his eyes wide and staring. Mine. To have and to hold. A rhythm, a timelessness. Spinning into his arms and out again. I will not let you go. How could I ask you to love me when you loved her still? The thrill of his touch against my skin. This I did with her, and this, and this. And his kiss, this kiss and this one, mine.

XVII

Here she is. Summoned up. Eyes flashing, she takes shape and form before me, slashing at her horse, seizing life with her two hands. She looks down on us. Triumphant, leaning down from the minstrel's gallery with a smile on her lips. Making an entrance into the quiet scene. Amused by this clumsiness. Shrinking away from her. *I don't want to look back on those years, I don't want even to tell you about them.* How tenuous my grip on malice. Beauty, it's all due to her. Sensing the depth of his disgust. I want him to go on talking like this, that his bitterness might loosen and come away. That ugly laughter. Sweeping us aside. Her puppets.

Anamaría Crowe Serrano

on first reading Stuart Kendall's *Gilgamesh*

spasms   because
you move the maenad in me[1]

        tongue
     between your toes
     slow curl under
        paleolithic suck

these garments in the later paintings   wispy
veils and want-want weave   are too
             dreary
   dead as sleep in Nineveh[2]

     I've ripped them up   gauzy arabesque
of the type you imagined
     in your weaker moments
          might be
        pulled off a shoulder
        teased away to please
              reveal...

---

[1] we can make this
        tomorrow's fetish   we must

[2] http://en.wikipedia.org/wiki/Nineveh

y aaaaa wn

my mouth
cannot
be naked
any
wider

i'm off to ride the bull   if not slay it
        before hunting your gods

                    who said love is like a red red[3] rose...
                        it is
                        and there's the rub

                    we need a good secateurs

        i digress   the real garment
is not wispy gauze but woven with my pubic hair[4]
                the primitive joy of it
                against your thighs and your crotch

            your hands chained
                    behind the chair

---

[3] so clichéd   and Neruda's poetry is over-rated too
[4]   Bethesda
    houses your civility   healing
                    is irrelevant after this

it's woven to the crenellations

where we left the castle tour

to rewrite the untouched histories

of nooks   hidden places[5]

where we could be

mythical   animal

where *cunt* and *prick* and *fuck*

are not pejorative

the silken milk-and-honey bollocks

in the later paintings of the maenads

    burns the painter's brush

    their buttocks is worthy of more

                more realism

    rubbing off Bacchus' godly stubble

    proper burlap chin   rubble upper lip

        red red real[6]

    their juices[7] dripping lava over his face

        melting his tongue

    their lungs a feckless howl[8]   shredding sheets

        the way storms strip

        the sky

            deflower

            the forest

---

[5] in full view
[6] / love doesn't come into it
[7] is there another word for that?
[8] think Ginsberg

Peter Boyle

Gaston Bousquin visits Olga Orozco in her Buenos Aires apartment, late summer 1981

She eyes the aquarium with its one remaining fish
and intones in the voice of the cat: "*Tú reinaste en Bubastis.*"
She goes under the water of her tiny aquarium
and hides there, goby-like, under the greyest rock.
She is invisible, knitted into
the long caul of her days.
When she returns, full-woman-size, through the front door
she takes a thin slip of paper
from a box of dreams by the broom closet
and watches the green and purple twists of smoke
rising from its pyre. In the crook of her arm,
on the white tips of her fingers,
lie traces of that shimmering light
things bring with them from the time
they first moved out of water. Exiles in the strange land
of carbon and air. She is a deity
of the other world. Through the sunken
eye of a rock-face, down the spiral of chiselled
steps she precedes me, the taut sway
of her African kaftan grazing the stone,
into the tropic garden of my future.
I am destined always
to misunderstand her, to
misrepresent her, to be a small carrier
of her transmuted inoperable virus.
She reincarnates and is born backwards
among her Irish and Italian ancestors.
Even perched on this sumptuous chair,
she feels puncturing her face
the stones that will lie above her grave.
Though I am talking to her in my halting Spanish
I already feel her presence

in the houseboat I will rent on Middle Harbour
and her smile, her shyness is there
waiting like a second shadow to greet me
beside the gruff Immigration Officer
at Friday Harbor. She is present
in the cigar that stuns me and weaves
circles of trance in my expensively imported head.
I walk out onto a balcony over a gully
and she is sitting there, nursing a cat—
it finds the hidden milk behind her long-dry nipple.
I sit in the chair opposite.
Neither of us can find words.
We both know what it is to come from the moon.
"Continue walking," she says to me without speaking.
"It is your destiny to walk to Patagonia.
Once you reach its final rocks you must pledge
always to stay south of the Equator.
You are not destined to find any home—
settling anywhere would prematurely tilt
the balance of your cerebellum into some
wayward dash into death.
Never trust the algorithms. Place yourself securely
in the isolated helm of going under.
Keep your eyes fully open
as the vampire insects of the cosmos swarm towards you.
Trust this solitude and what it says to you,
this reticent tongue-tied intelligence
that moves only in singularities.
Gleaned from what is much older than human,
recite the authentic contours of falling.
And now to cross this bridge of arsenic, as we say.

"Choose
but don't cheat, don't whisper any counter-spell,
any words of return."

The Mass of the West Wind

for William Cliff

glory to those who dwell
in the silences of the world
in the hull of the tramp steamer
in the cargo freighter's oil and rust, the narrow cabin
hole in the wall of darkness
this bitter unglorified monastic cell
afloat in an ocean with no gods

glory to those who have rested in honesty
in the places where there is nothing
where evil has shaped its sharp
enduring scar—
lifeless avenues, spectral streets,
bars where no one risks crying or touching
or speaking anymore

glory to those who persist
in places where there are no words no images
no consolatory swirls of rhetoric
where to stay for five days
is to know the circle Dante
was too frightened to describe

glory to those who impose on the world
only the openness of their eyes
their truth
to each face of suffering
their tiny drained
willingness to be there

The Well

Far below in the valley
a small light glitters—
the pilot light of the underworld
shining from the earth-bound well
where my mother lives.

I am at the airport waiting for my cousin to arrive
bringing the sealed urn with the elixir
direct from Florida.
We will sprinkle it over her face:
ageing will stop, she will grow young again
and we will pour what remains in the urn
over the ashes of our house
and it will come back:
my brothers and I will be sitting there
at the long table,
around us space will hang
suspended for one moment
as paint grows back, laughter ricochets above us,
buried tins of long-lost regrets
reappear in cupboards—

and a single peal of my mother's voice
will be there
sounding in the ear of each of us—
her voice
like flakes of bread made golden in a light
unknown to any of us
will settle into the deep furrows
over the eyebrows of each of our children
while our own voices chase

the whirlwind of dust.

Norman Jope

Nightfall

The volcano's shadow hushes birds
on this late spring evening. Spread out in its wake
is a succulent country with its myriad fields.
It is still all there to be eaten
and my life is so brief that I mourn and celebrate
this fact as I sit on a hill in the Auvergne
by the power of remote viewing, listening hard
to the final evensongs of tiny birds
and in love with the tiles of isolated farms
and pungent herbs the colour of stars.
Mortal in the face of earth and sky and gods
who withhold their blessings, yet persist
on the far side of cloud, I consider my words...
and what remains is the passage of a mind
through time, to nakedness and numbness,
an absence into which the fading song
will fall, as if into a well, as the green volcano
merges its shadow with the night.
At the end of this longest of days, I am dumbstruck
by my strangeness, by the magic of my brevity,
by my life so singular and uncanny
that somehow it seems mythical,
no matter how mundane—and perhaps, I think,
it is you that dreamt me as I watch the stars come out
in a darkening space that arches over Europe,
and, perhaps, that space will contain us
in our deaths as in our lives, in an afterlife of birdsong
and pipistrelles darting, beating winged hands in the dark.
For now, however, the birds are hushed.
More mortal than benighted, I am backlit by death.

An Old Vocation in a New City

He sees himself stepping out, at ease with the crowds at the entrance,
past the snack-stands and news-stalls, delving into the metro,
heading for the centre, as if there were ever such a thing
on a spherical world. He sees himself with his usual hunger
for places, faces, spaces, the delirious sensations of life—
its flavours and favours, its spices and nostrums
make up the map of his desire, a map he is still unfolding
and will see him through to his journey's end.
There are too many cities, too many feasts and too many loves
for a single life. He loves it all, including all that he hates,
precisely because it will desert him, or he unwillingly desert it
and this, for his generation, deprived of the immortality
that human consciousness deserves, is the nature of the bargain—
here, so vividly here now, it will all be gone in a matter of years
and he can only shrug at that, as he sits at a pavement café,
planning the day ahead, if not in too much detail,
as the coffee cools to an ideal temperature
and the world accepts him, as death on this day does not.

Isobel Armstrong

Three Lamps and their Bases

1
golden dragon swells round
the blood-red bulge
of the lamp-base as
eye smooths a gleam
in the glaze touch
sees the cool crimson's contour
gilded scales thrash

2
butterfly
wings webbed in gold
embedded in enamel cinnabar
and symmetries of lotus flower
carmine white and carmine
among scrolls of green

four folded companions
embossed at each corner
among tendrils of lotus flower
those winged eyes
blue-pearl pearl-pink pink-pearl pearl-blue
unable to flutter
but ever on the watch
fix their sealed looks in pigment
pearled gold-ribbed wings
eyes
unbruised by any gaze

3
in
deep azure

just beyond the lamp's curvature
a half-seen bird of
paradise dives for cherries as
blossom surfs golden boughs
in a flush of orange – pattern rhymes
over and over
daisy carnation peony peony carnation daisy
gold-veined petals
cascade from a basket of flowers
incised on deep blue
on which a basket of flowers
is incised where cas
cade orange-flushed petals threaded
with gold   where in the rounded surface's beyond
birds of paradise alight
to bite cherries
a flower just might
from out the deep blue azure fall
out of the order of things
with a ceramic chink
on the table
on

Oriental Rug

crimson scarlet vermilion
names for red
glow in worn hieroglyphs
scarlet foot-trodden ciphers
ancient forgotten vermilion codes   unread
incarnadine threads   now
just the hermeneutics of red
old vermilion scarlet crimson

now   here   now
in torsion

leads   flex   cable
twist across carpet-scape's crimson
spread unseen networks of messages
keep the secrets of cyber space
now
modem Cyclops in triplicate
flickering vertical eyes
signals for the virtual world
innocently says
nobody tricked you
nobody

Fruitbowl

almost translucency buried
in grape green   skin presses
on apple's flush heavy
against pear's yellow gold contours   membrane
cut with minuscule brown grazes sprinkled brown pores

Peter Boyle & M.T.C. Cronin

from Guidelines for New People: Anti Commentaries

Cosmology

There are five parallel worlds and they drift seamlessly across each other. On the first world household objects float unencumbered by expectations, the dog not quite on the mat, the mat rippling off the stone floor, the sink gliding by talking to the water. Cups and saucers circulate, the dead tenderly brushing the shoulders of the living. On the next world speed and grief transfer their energies, while joy sifts slowly downward, the precipitate of ripeness. Threatening to outweigh the others, there is the blue world where light seeps towards the erasure end of the spectrum. In the smallest of the worlds anger and pain pound against enclosed walls. No exit. The fifth world cannot yet be described. It awaits its language. Of it they say, "Let your heart learn openness."

Commentary

As an inhabitant of the smallest world I must ask why you have written *Cosmology*. I have been swatting flies for many histories and can find no reason why. There has never been a way out of not understanding.

Astrology

The sign of the bumblebee. The sign of the fly. The sign of the two year old boy. The sign of the five year old boy. The sign of the hellish mother. The sign of the fly catcher. The two year old boys have the job of the world. A dendritic system. Like the mind as it designs a brain. Designed to take itself off. Remove signs. The flower has no sign. The stars have been falling into it forever. Don't mislook at or misread the signals. Among you are the stars. You are among. Whose left hand? Whose right? The fly is very easily caught sideways.

Commentary

As an inhabitant of a small world where the only fate is a collective fate (viz world disappearance) I fail to understand the fascination with a multitude of individualised signs. Unless stars read their own signs. Unless the flower, demanding a sign, falls into the world of anger.

Luminosity

There are voices in the sun's lights on the water. But they are voices which do not speak. You can feel them in your forehead if you listen hard. They are grey but not like shadows because everywhere is dark. If you want to hear these voices you should expand your chest. When it is as wide as all the silence they will enter you together with every sound. Then the lights of the sun will tell you what they told the water. Something the water did not hear.

Commentary

What you cannot hear, was it ever meant for your hearing? When the chest is expanded to the four directions, the voice disappears.

What you cannot speak, is it the buzz of the fly that has already spoken you?

Diluvianism

Before the deluge there were more records of the worlds. The black genoa fig and the brown turkey fig were listed. So were the long lives of the dead. Harvests were noted and on worlds where they were not needed patterns were classified and duly catalogued. If a world existed with only a single pattern ingenuity filled the record books alongside tibrons and platypussaries and nomadidae and a people called the Laz. There were scribed leading men and leading ladies; leach-men and laymen. What could fill the lists went far beyond the worlds themselves. But only one thing surpassed the flood of all worlds. How they were thought of.

Commentary

In silence stands the list of the enduring. Not named and not thought of. The maelstrom of what no one noticed. Before and after flood.

Trajectory

Every night you get up, cook breakfast, go out to shop. You drive slowly in your sleep, wearing your flannel pyjamas. We go from shop to shop as you hunt the always elusive ingredients for the dinners your grandmothers made years ago asleep in other countries. I walk beside you, seeking to avoid arguments for the law is not kindly to couples engaged in violent public altercations as they sleep. Soon he arrives—your brother, your boyfriend, I'm never sure which. It's hard shopping with the dead always wanting to add in their commentary, still it's something that must be done when life takes place in reverse between midnight and dawn. You insist on a jog through the park. The moon continues its trajectory from east to west yet you travel steadily north in your sleep, towards lakes in sub-Arctic forests, wind-grazed tundras. We come to the always open airport and read off the destinations we plan to go one day when everything will change. With you as dawn approaches I climb back into bed. I watch as one by one the pages I have written go blank, taking back the life I lived for twenty years watching over your sleep. I will never clean up the trashed streets that lie in our wake. Love goes on striking us down and claiming us.

Commentary

I am getting tired of watching over you as you sleep.

The Social Contract

In the narrow downstairs bathroom seven rats harmoniously inhabit the bathtub. Three more are already sampling the varied forms of soap, trying out the locks to the razor cabinet. Their combined activity in governing the household is impressive. Attuned to distant wars and invasions they regulate their koinos with rules ducktaped to the lightbulb. In the shaving mirror the reflection of a TV left running informs them of humanity's progress. The exploding towns trouble them but mostly they worry what strange foods secreted in oval bowls fuel the vendettas of a vanishing race.

Commentary

When the philosophers voyaged in a small saucer across the very grimy soapslick that is called Apprising Yesterday, they took little notice of the darkness that bled from their fingers. No one said, 'What you least want to reveal is already lapping distant galaxies, already builds the silt of our everyday shore.'

Reproduction

It has been suspected by those who map everything but never read the maps of themselves that all the worlds give birth to each other. So a tea-party can give rise to the sky and arch-poets can argue shades of blue. You might laugh at this if it is on another world that you drop to sleep at night but if yet another world is born while you dream annoying guns might wake in you the language of pure power. Speak this and what grows will jump out of the box just like jack.

Commentary

Before sleeping, tend flowers carefully that they do not abandon you to the invisible ocean. Be wary of words that grow too large. Leave the shades of the sky alone: their lives are busy enough minding the cosmos.

Dialect

This building where I sleep is made entirely of explosives. All night they have been shelling South Lebanon, Gaza and Beirut, Haifa and portions of Iraq, towns in Afghanistan and villages in Ingoshetia they won't ever tell us about. In this glorious war the dead have only one language and it is Pitjanjara-Arabic, Hebrew-Russian, not forgetting Kurdish-Armenian Angolan, and the simple dialect of everyone. In a vast airport the dead arrive wanting to sleep on safe soil. All the Presidents keep firing but the dead won't stop at the barriers. The smiles of these TV men stammer: 'Keep these people away from me—I've levelled their cities—don't they know when to quit.'

Commentary

The simple dialect of everyone contains only five words: 'we will kill them all'. But we still don't know what 'all' is referred to.

Tim Dooley

After Herrick

I was delivering
with what talent,
verve or conviction
I could muster
some element
no doubt of the
heritage strand
of the National
Curriculum (revised),
when a Julia
or Celia took from
her pencil case
a handful of coloured
markers and started
to construct log fences
or oxers—delicate,
suspended by their
own weight—on
the desk in front
of her. Absorbed
by the task and with
half an ear open
no doubt to Juliet's
fate, she inhabits
a bubble of youth
I would not burst,
that time's transhifting
has failed to wear away.

According to John

i

He was playing with one of the birds outside the house,
a partridge maybe, or guinea fowl, *chuck-chuck-chukar*
-chukar it sang; and he crouched throwing seeds to it.
And one of the militia passing on patrol jeered,
Is that how you scholars pass the time? And he said,
looking up at them in the jeep—Didn't the Greeks
say the bird was like a soul?—and—What do any of us
do that's different from digging around in the dust?

Questions. It was always questions with John.

ii

Then there was the story about the bugs. We were
supposed to sleep on pallets in a rough outhouse,
part of a consciousness-raising tour or something.
Yusuf was complaining about bites in the night.
All of us were cold and in need of a wash. And
John put on a grand voice saying—Bugs. Keep
away from us. This mission is sacred. We laughed
and finally got some rest. In the morning he pointed
to the door where the bugs were bunched together.
Was that where the last of the honey was spilled?
He pointed—How creatures obey the voice of a man
when men disobey the commands of their god.

Passive-aggressive, or what?

iii

So the ship, he said, is only safely home
when it comes into the harbour's water

ahead of the storm. And the crop can be
counted on when its harvest is stored in the barn.
The athletes can be proud on the rostrum,
when their medals are fairly won.

Until then, count the risks.

Sadness, the love you have for your children,
your parents' needs, ambition, lack of money,
praise from friends, your youth and health,
beauty, vanity, desire, too much wealth,
short temper, settled hate, promotion,
inertia, idleness, envy of others, possessiveness,
timidity, self-righteous cheek, dishonesty,
did I mention money? the wrong kind of love,
pretentiousness, bad faith...

The obstacles are legion.

Better to enjoy the trip, I thought.

iv

And he could hate well enough.
When the news came of what they'd done
to the body of the girl they killed,
he started giving names to them—
piss-stench, sewer-spewer,
rotten flesh, foul flame-fruit,
tree of burning coals,
dark from within the madness of matter,
neighbour of cancer,
stranger to the holy bath.

We were with him on that.

v

When he talked of his Master, it was never the same.
That was the point, he said.
Sometimes his skin looked soft as a girl's,
though the chest was firm and smooth
when I rested my head there.

James said the Master was like a child,
or a youth with a new beard.
No, said John, the beard was thick and flowing
and on top his hair was already receding.
How the light shone back at us from the wise wide forehead.

vi

When they took him in, John said,
I was scared and ran away.
Holed up in a cave in the hills for a while.
Then in the half-light a figure came.
That wasn't me they got, said the Master.
That was the other man you sometimes glimpsed.
That was a cross of wood, but this is a cross of light.

John pointed to the sky and talked
like some scientist from CERN
about energy and matter and light,
wholeness and singularity,
the root of things, the left hand and the right.

vii

And that's how it was in those days,
we'd sit on the steps of that old ruin
near Selçuk and listen to traveller's tales.
There was the one we called Sun-Ra,

the no-meat man, back from his overland trip
to Kabul, Lahore and all points East.
There are many gods he'd say
but only one source of light.
Care for each other, like these sparrows do.

So it was in those days
by the old temple of Artemis.
And some of us dressed like those men.
Some of us followed their diets.
Some of us learned their rites
or wrote out their sayings.
Some followed their words hoping to better their lives.
Some used their power to enslave.

viii

He was playing with one of the birds outside the house,
a partridge maybe, or guinea fowl, *chuck-chuck-chukar*
-chukar it sang; and he crouched throwing seeds to it,
stroked and ruffled its feathers. One of the patrol passing
asked, Is that how you wise men pass the time?
He looked over at them, That rifle over your shoulder,
do you always keep it cocked and ready to shoot?

I don't remember what he answered,
but the fighting goes on.

Michael Farrell

Singing

To understand. Realisations in the shower
Now I've sung your story I know about the
Shifts in voice—it isn't all one perspective

    Ahh Ahhh Ahhhh

A saying isn't said just because it sounds good
It's broad-humoured, yet can be said plain in
Front of children; if you sing it even better

    Ahhhh Ahhh Ahh

You know one thing about a song from
The radio. You know something else when
It's coming from your own throat—that's
The note. A song doesn't belong on a page
A song isn't on it like paint. A song, a
Page make structure, make place, thing. A
Thing that can do and change and be ruined
You know that door doesn't belong to a woman
Or a man, it's rather everything you're leaving
Everything you're running to. But you sing it
Like a drowning or a jumping up through a trap
Door and it's yours. Sit down, there's a guitar
On the fire—it plays no good but it burns beaut
Ifully. Didn't you have a love like that? A life
Weren't you born here or close enough or far
Away? Didn't you drink enough wine to make
You doubt it could stand in for anything but it
Self? It was all too general, too general, too
Universal, we didn't want it, we didn't want
Anything that way, not like a novel, not like
An allegorical painting of Hope or Victory

Let that kind of suffering belong to those times
Let it all be the blinding drift of good after
Noons and nights that were just a movie of
The moon. We wanted to be—we were—shel
Tered. The song we sang then was about a dog
That had gone wild and its character was com
Plex and it saved someone's life in an unexpec
Ted way… and we didn't die: we took a good
Hard look at our lives in the words we sang
It was a joy. The song itself was the girl, the
Boy, the dance, the stimulation. It just had
Too much class to make it explicit. The song
Had moves that took us where we weren't
Supposed to go (we supposed). And we
Looked around, it was the night, the trees

And the words had changed. We ate the burnt
Guitar because we thought that's what you do

The Bon Vieux Temps

He was nothing new (that's why we liked him). He was a
    good French
bushman who wouldn't betray a Christian—should you decide
    to treat him
like a gently nurtured dame leaping blackberry canes. Toujours
    gai: now
the abode en permanence has arrived and nights like champagne
    cream fall
distinctly on the ear. We would abstract body parts like that
    then (star
illimitable, ocean-brightened). It was Arabian on the beach.
    Molonglo
took the bungalow while I lay openmouthed under the gooseberries.
    We didn't
call them lady adjuncts then and didn't need to. We thanked
    Allah for
the caravanserai or fountain of youth. And it could all go on
    with a black
boy to help with the accounts but what if we decentred Rolf
    Boldrewood's
sentiments and looked where we were headed, to WWI, for
    example.
It was natural to be involved like strawberries in a washing
    machine,
if strawberries were innocent of being colonial: but that's hardly
    possible
their tendrils get in everywhere.

Heidi Williamson

Newton's Rings

                Difficult to make out
         in this still   black and white
            sonogram   if the halo
            surround   on your shining
            bones is a   light shadow
            thrown by   the instrument,
         like a coffee   stain in reverse, or
         your mini   sea as it laps
          around your   form. Difficult
          too, to imagine   you, inside me,
          in full colour.   It's only
            as you emerge   through the
            difficult prism   of birth
                that your   colours
                astonishingly graduate

Hellbox

My mother had two mouths. One was for saying.
The other was for not saying. She kept a budgerigar
padlocked in a tarnished cage in the attic. At dusk
she would climb to the top of the house with a
lime green feather boa on her bony resurrected
shoulders. She would sing to the bird and watch
its confusion. Later, she would preen it with her
bird-cat tongue. She would tell it: Listen, can't you?
After all this, someone, somewhere still calls out to
me in prayer.

Peter Robinson

Street-Combing

for O.

Sun's setting behind us at 5 pm;
a turquoise stripe below a rain front
strokes in sudden severance,
as does the sunshine after rain.
We're out street-combing once again,
out along the pavement's edge
for snippets, abject filaments
of telephone junction-box wire.

You have your cloth-bag for each object:
packing tape, blue or yellow twine
towards up-cycled basketwork...
I've got the bits of scribbled paper
and now, back in my element,
can hear the tug of spoken words,
their ebb and flow between us
'on a day to honour', as you said.

It's a day with rain clouds up ahead,
but also sunshine after rain
picking out pale green mildew
luminous on a wintry bough,
making the white house opposite glow.
Belisha beacons flash their orange
and I'm struck by all this perseverance
as you stoop for one more *Merzbau*
scrap of stuff beneath my notice,
love, lifting it into the light.

Weather Events

We had stepped out for a breath of air
and as if on the edge of a blind precipice,
had strode across the sodden meadow.
You were giving me some good advice.
The news might mean our world is dying,
dying with us, but without us too
on one more perishing January day.
Still I caught birdsong this morning
and the good man doesn't brood on death,
nor avoid the thought, come to think of it.
But something rotten below the bridge,
a swollen drain, some stagnant water
brought that every third thought back
to each depredation of predator and prey.

Swans were struggling against the current.
Their element so far extended
they splashed about the roots of trees.
The river paths impassable at points;
yet we had walked out to survey
this flooding of the valley floor.
White seagulls rose up from its waters.
The flights of locks were good as useless:
torrents overwhelmed sluices, gates,
the run-offs skimmed with waste and slime.
So much was driven down in the flow
of extreme events now, well, I ask you,
if you're giving me some good advice,
how do I treasure what we have to let go?

Anywhere on Thames

Look, here, a bandstand in the flood!
Islanded, its water music,
rippling forward, orchestrates
this sunken scene.
                    You notice
a swan's neck craning for wet crusts
near the children's muddy feet
by water, rained-on water lapping
everywhere in a municipal park
and the parkland's stricken landscape
shines from torn-patched blues of sunlight
intermittently.
                    Marbling reflections
of that shimmer on the ripples
are painted over paddling garden
sculptures, churchyard headstones,
a stranded roundabout and swing,
the house-wall lichen, mosses, leaflets
of its pioneers.
                    We're all in this together
now, gone out after lunch to see
how high water levels reach
with the bare and threatened tree-
roots undermined, up-rooted, borne
down towards a weir.
                    Advancing
figures, low light behind them,
are silhouettes fringed in an aura of sun,
their wind-gust-flustered hair a halo
and the very idea aglow.

So to Speak

'There will not be books in the running brooks
until the dawn of hydro-semantics.'
　　　　　—J. L. Austin

'A fact that I would beg you to discuss.'
　　　　　—Kurt Schwitters

So to speak out of the flowing water
strolled by in a winter's dark
is almost more than you can bear,
speaking of water gone under the bridge
as it courses into mid-town,
swirling and boiling down there
over each lock-gate and overfull channel
seeking its level in you, so to speak,
inches from where at the towpath
and carrying other grief too
from a bereavement's aftermath
(oh spare us the details, it as good as says)
you can hear those waters bring
turmoil, reddish-brown mud
deposited over a children's play area
as it floods, floods past canal barges
moored to hibernate by the white cottages,
their weeping willows in earliest bud,
and tells you, so to speak,
there's no more truth left to be told,
what's past is past, it didn't matter,
the stuff that might have happened then
(and too much happened, said or unsaid),
tells you in the water's own words
not to expect a reply, so to speak,
although you know there's no such thing...

Vicarious Light

The five of us sat at a table for six,
there's nobody opposite me;
and I'm not inclined to think it lain
for anyone, even you.

But such thoughts aren't quite kept at bay
by light in the restaurant window,
its gleam and shadow lines
projected, noir-like, across a white wall
from slatted wooden blinds.

Orders arriving before you'd have fretted,
riverside airiness shines
in filled glasses and flower-vase petals
as if from motes would fall
nothing resembling sorrow,
remorse, things regretted,
for, no,

all this sunlight has dazzled them away.

Damian Furniss

1928   Tirana, Albania

King Zog

When the Prime Minister
declared himself President
the President decreed
he be crowned king—
planes rained confetti,
sheep were slaughtered,
two thousand men freed,
two hundred hung.

His palace was superior
to a second string casino
in any minor Belgian resort,
its guest bedrooms
wanting for nothing
but distinguished guests.

The valley men wished
a plague of blind bears
on the men of the valleys—
they needed a strong man
to keep them together,
to hold them apart.

When a would-be assassin
pulled a pistol on him
Zog drew his golden gun,
took aim and fired,
pinning silver medals
with scarlet ribbons
into his assailant's chest,
the ash undisturbed
on his perpetual cigarette.

The Mighty Line

'Our playgrounds echo with unborn children.
The mothers of the lost are grey and barren.
Not all men who returned from the last war—
and we here have much to thank them for—
returned from the war they won as men.
My friends, this must never happen again!'
Monsieur Maginot unrolls his master plan,
sketches trenches in the air, baton in hand:
'Here, the last line of attack,' he fences
a ghost, 'must be the first line of defence.'

'Beneath six feet of concrete, Generals,
your mess undisturbed by uninvited shells,
chefs shall enjoy the cool of a kitchen
fully equipped with air-conditioning.'
They raise a toast to the Lion of Verdun
with a Riesling bottled in the Saar Basin,
resolve to reshape the land between Alps
and Ardennes, that the Boches be corralled
in their tanks, hoiked out like snails,
to amuse the mouth with beurre à l'ail.

Salt of the Earth

'In the time of our elders,
back in Britisher time,
the Mahatma walked
the ghats of Ahmedabad
to the flat pans of Dandi,
took the salt of the sea
in the palm of his hand,
offered it to a country
that was yet to be born.'

Our guide wears khadi
from his cap to his dhoti,
hot steps their march
into a thicket of lathis,
mimes the head blows
of steel-tipped bo sticks
the length of saplings
wielded by striplings
clad in webbed khaki.

'And here is his statue
carved out of saltstone
to remember that time:
last year men came
and thumbed out his eyes,
left him face down
in the watering hole,
licked at by buffalo
and buzzing with flies.'

In the Name of the Father

He has the yellow ache
and caves around his eyes;
something, some thing moves
in the crowd of his insides
and he reaches for the milk
to anaesthetise the pain
dancing round his study
like a bear on a chain.

He calls for People's Houses
as once palaces were raised
so Turks may read God's word
in the language they pray in,
a space to have their visions
and have their visions realised,
make an art for the future—
the future in the skies.

When they give him his name,
elect him Father of the Nation,
he takes his name as a father
takes a gift from his children:
asks that all his pictures
be hung skewed when he's gone
that the people be reminded
of all he did right doing wrong.

The House of Saud

In the beginning was the House of Saud. And then came the kingdom. And then its king. And the king laid claim to the sand, every grain of it. And the wadis also, for there things grow.

And all the land became theirs. And all that lies beneath the land. And all that is raised upon it. All that flies above the land is now theirs also, and all that crawls below it.

The holy cities are theirs by decree. And the holy places of the holy cities. And all the pilgrims who make their pilgrimage to those holy places. And the taxes on all those pilgrims spend there.

And those who resist, they shall be beheaded in the four cities. And their heads shall be displayed from the high places in every corner of the thirteen provinces. For in the desert, bad seeds do not grow.

And from one king shall spring seven thousand princes. And each of those seven thousand princes, they shall have no more than four wives at once, and do their duty to each, as is decreed.

And the princes shall be given sinecures and stipends. And with those sinecures shall come great palaces. For princes begat princes, each with a mouth to feed and feet to shod.

And those sons of princes shall marry the daughters of priests. And the sons of priests shall marry the daughters of princes. And they shall rule under heaven and over earth.

For theirs is the kingdom, reflecting its glory, for all men. As it has been, and is now, it shall always be. So long as there are stars in the night sky, and the moon sings blue silver to the trees.

Paula Bohince

Acrostic: Charred and Luminous

Charcoal briquettes imitate shadowy mice the owl
hunts, only crumbling over fire instead of shredding in a talon.
A minor difference. Meanwhile, our rabbit stews in the BBQ. Serve it
rare. In smoke twists exploits of its bones.
Radiant baby, fat like moonlight in the pan's dented corners,
edged silver turning black.
Designs come. We interpret them, grate
Asiago, grind peppercorns. Loose rabbits won't do.
Nests are ungovernable. One of our brothers stages a coup:
delves into brush with a sack and a hammer,
litter removed from the mother, mother the star of our supper
under this lunar eclipse (how lucky!). Sky
minus moon equals an occasion not to be missed, a pinhole helmet.
Icarus himself would have laid down wings to see it.
Nothing in the sky to guide our eyes, the ahhs and
oohs a type of funeral song. Don't be sad. Grill the meat,
undercook it. I know how you want it: soft, buttered,
salted. Eat it in the dark before the moon comes back, by crescents.

Homing Pigeons, In Absentia

How we came to hate them,
snug in the blossoming pear, doubling
its womanliness with their
flirtatious genius—elusive, unpossessed,
unresponsive when our widower
neighbor signaled them.

Yours now, he said.

Pink-cheeked, lent the illusion of
satiety, youth, they studied us
all spring, which we longed for
to end, then through summer's freight
of frightened minutes,

intuiting us: soberly eyeing our bed-
room and boxes. Perceptive as children,
stunned on the branches.

Hornet Spring

The pump handle's loose with thaw.
Water hears its high call.
A trumpet clambers to the spout's lip,
dazzled by a melting shine.
The signal is lost, frantic dance
of danger forgotten.
Those who escape with a wave
on their wings fly the flag of their lives
over strip-mined fields.
Those who are patient tumble inside
the gloss, fall like slower water.

Anne Gorrick

The New Sentence

for Ron Silliman

The dematerialization of writing
took place in my kitchen
The postindustrial experience is difficult
as an interior poetic structure
always semantically given
in Multi-channel Installation Fullscreen
This is a breathtaking event
with underlined content

When do you become eligible for parole under "the New Sentence?"

Exhausted from our long journey
we decided to go straight to bed
Click on the New Sentence button
Any omission is pointless
So, I've gone back, used the backspace key to remove spaces
before the new sentence, and add only one space

The new sentence—which could be the same as the old sentence— is
scheduled to be imposed on Friday

Your sentence lacks a subject
The new sentence is outright "unlawful"
You must start a new sentence
more or less ordinary
with a curious niggling apropos
with no specific referential focus
with heavy kinetic stress
theoretical hesitations
This probably has most to do
with a very strong feeling that telling stories

actually is an idea of history
that shudders with a gorgeous sets
broken apart by signs of equivalence

The new sentence is an investigation
a navigator of the labyrinth
a word as commodity
The alphabet gap has lodged unasked
in some vague after light

The night of the trial, angered relatives of the young men kidnap
Silliman, take him to occupied New York, and sentence him to hang

There is electrophysiological evidence
of disrupted sentence processing
of mimetism and montage
that aim to disrupt existing forms
Repeat these sentences, with slight alterations and rearrangements
When they were pried loose
these tears often thwart the reading of a complete word or sentence
torqueing the theory of existence

Albany to show us what's underneath
the summer death... the bark in the sentences of dogs
that awful brown fence
I caught her in mid-sentence
These verbs mirror relations of natural force
in the household of God
refer to the new creation
while your nook automatically
inserts new text into the preceding stanza
to double the sentence count

These are spare unraveled acts of attention
It took an entire document
(if that was what it took)
to get rid of one discordant-sounding sentence
This is why I write a sentence like the second one before this one

In the pressure chambers, there are echoes
I like to think of it as a day of recognition
Various other actions arise ex delicto
All variants drop the word "the" before "science"
I wrote this sentence with a ballpoint pen
Seminal grandstanding in charismatic direct
Leave out the verbs
Screw up the narrative
No Other Sentence Could Have Followed but This

Now the students have to redraw their pictures to match the new
sentence

The Alchemical Kitchen

"Where is my hay? Where is my benzoin? Where is my cypress?"
"I knew I had to learn aromatherapy if I couldn't see a doctor for three years."
         —Charlotte Mandell

My milk, my guru, my tea
Where is
my water, my heart, my bus
Where is my jelly, my mind
my boy, my warfleet, my gnome
my hope, my library, my Excedrine

Have you ever lost your phone?
Ever had one stolen?
Do you worry about these things?
What if you could get it back?

Here is the future you've been dreaming about with ray guns,
robot maids, unisex jumpsuits

Your appendix, your god, your wilderness
Where is
my watershed, my country, my gigantic bone machine

Where is
your treasure, your field, your body, your sweet spot mileage
your god chord, your diaphragm, your mouth and its cherries
Where is your rupture?

Where is
her hand going next?
Circe would destroy the world
Where is
her hair, her jealous sugar daddy, her exact location
OH GOD WHERE IS HER SKIN
Her sense of proportion, her bra, her crapazoid fanfic

   (a) What kind of mirror is this?
   (b) Where is her face relative to the radius of curvature or focal
            length?
   (c) What is the radius of curvature of the mirror in cm?

Her wardrobe, her groom, her cleverness, her stuff
Where is her room located, her engagement ring, her grave

(The second form somewhat redundantly and nonsensically asks
about the location of a position)

(Use the arrow keys and the spacebar to shoot)

Where is
his critical thinking, his glory, his other sock
his birthmark, his attorney, his new skin
his equivalent, his miracles, his neck, his hometown
Where is his amputated arm buried?

You can post anything from anywhere
But The Next Person Who Pisses In A Bottle Is Fired

At what time in the summer do the redwings disappear from the
            swamps?
Where do they gather in flocks?
Where is their special feeding ground?

Their argument, their relationship, their gold,
their spot, their warm debris
WHERE IS THEIR DUST AND WHY
Their evidence, their customer service, their jungle
Their deceptively light-sounding consensus

Where is their lament for the loss of the Merchant in lightening at
        Pigeon Hole?
Where is their land?
Where is their ivory, their right of rank?
Where are their laborers and the gardens they tended?
Centurians might be known Christians
standing breathless
as circus victims panic
stuck in Scream Arena butchery
55% of commuters drink Coca Cola and/or Johnnie Walker Black
        Label and use AXE deodorant
35% drink Nescafé

You can tell them to use a certain color bandage
made out of his laundry
to cure this disappointed picture

Jeremy Hooker

Hurst Castle

'It's very special how there are ways, a field, a place, where our
deepest creative concerns connect.' —Noah Pikes

1

Dear friend,
you have sent my mind racing,
skipping the years.

2

You will know how the sea
runs up among the stones,
how it laps and lapses,
surges with the tide.
And wind whips off the foam.
And the Shingles buoy's bell rings.

Behind us, granite walls,
concrete, brick, rusted steel doors
clamped shut on cannon mouths.

A symbol of power,
once our playground,
empty as a cockle shell.

3

Somehow this place is a way.
I feel I can talk to you through the walls.

4

Remember the Franciscan priest
immured here for thirty years?

A poor, infirm man, one side
of his body palsied,
how he would shuffle
in a dark, narrow room,
the only human sound
his jailor's tread. Other voices,
the sea's whisper or breaking crash,
a gull's cry.

So news of a far world came to him,
free voices,
which spoke of imprisonment.

5

Who were his brothers then?
And how could he bless?

6

Your voice, dear friend, was choked for years,
unknown as a foreign tongue,
locked in the throat.

At last, released,
it spoke a name that was new to you,
your name,
with a force opening the body's dark and narrow space.

7

You take me back.
So many fields, cities, countries.
And this is the place you bring me to—

This way
of wood and brick defences,
old jetties, the granite castle
with its giant weight of wars
an empty cockle shell.

Words bring me, your words,
words we have spoken to each other,
that connect us to a world.

Outside this narrow room in which I write,
inside, penetrating the walls,
I hear voices that speak of the sea.

Salisbury Cathedral: The Bust of Richard Jefferies

'I look at the sunshine and feel that there is no contracted order:
there is divine chaos, and, in it, limitless hope and possibilities.'
—Richard Jefferies

1

What is this man—

sad-eyed, with a beard
birds could nest in
if it weren't marble?

They brought him in
out of the wild,
refashioned him:
a Victorian worthy,
with a niche in the habitat
of bishops, burghers, and knights—

this man who disliked churches,
who found spires poking up

from cornland and downs
an offence,
who wished ruin on temples.

2

Would he seek refuge here today?

On Liddington Hill
he would hear the M4
and smell the fumes.
At Coate Water, estates move in.

Or say Wild England lives
where he knew it, in ditch
and field corner, where
I have seen it with his eyes?

3

If there has to be a statue
let it be one a bird can shit on,
something one can imagine
feeling the wind—

as I felt the wind blowing
through his words,
breaking images,
leaving knowledge
a heap of ruins, driving me
back from the known.

4

There are words
that scatter dead languages,
words that break
statues and statutes
that hide what is real.

This man walked out
of the life prepared for him,
smashed the marble forms.

He opened himself to chaos.
He lived by the quickest word.

It will not be petrified
by this absurdity.

Listen to the wind rising
among the monuments,

preparing to scatter them
like pieces of eggshell and leaves.

Julie Maclean

Bruthen Holocaust

Hurtling through rain
Lightning has struck
While ten k back
Fire in the bush
is out of control
Three red trucks
Sirens full wail
Ironic

It gets dark in a minute
Winds bend trees to the horizon
Gum leaves ping the windscreen
Hailstones threaten to pelt our bare faces

Road becomes river
and as we slow to stay afloat
the girl from the green campervan
parked across from us
Probably European
is squatting in the gravel
Her stream of piss
steaming in the sudden
fall in temperature
Air now freezing

Pale rare rump is pointed in our direction
Tempting a fork
that could skewer her to kebab
I reckon
My man and all the men, now curb crawling,
have something else on their minds

Bare flesh of arse
Black strappy top
Plaits of a fräulein

Lips that Did

He tempted me to his
idea of heaven
Honey oak Sixties writing desk
Essays on Rousseau, Voltaire
He got D's I recall
Spent hours at the mirror
trimming his Raleigh beard
Pinned a fabric print above the bed
of girls with Pre Raph hair
at some well in what could
have been Jai or Jodphur

He smoked every night
from a brown stained
Pipe he called Bong
Ash trays brimmed
with crimped stubs
or floated in beer

A flock couch, Deco attitude
Chunky, round about the arms
Like him, his favourite
Green
Rough on my stupid skin

Under his bed letters
from a Jezebel
Literature he tried to hide
where women took it
on the breasts, in the eyes
Dust, screwed up tissues

Under mine,
twenty streets away
Grubby northern sub
Thumbnail photos
Blue airmails
Ripped from opening, closing
Creased with love, longing
Wondering
What the hell I was doing *here*

Alasdair Paterson

My life with the pirates

Flag

What colours? To sail under? There's a question or two. Old salts favour a multiple choice, best kept in the flag locker snug as gunpowder, to be run up the mast at transmission time. Clue: the message is the mayhem. No codebook required. Our minimum recommendation:

The hourglass ultimatum
Anti-coagulant red
The compromised anatomy
Black spot bat flap
Crossed instruments of torture
The jolly event horizon

Plank

Timber, shivering. Fastidiousness of swabbed decks. Weapons to sharpen. Pressure to relieve. And always the sea, element we're on and out of, unaccountable, our bosom enemy. To propitiate.

So a rule change, a refinement in the game of wooden walls, after *stand by to repel, after strike your colours.* Bring it on, the loser's shaky forfeit, a one-way passage out, extruded claw of ship-substance that dangles, drops for sport, deeper than plummets sound, down and deep as krakens sleep. Or so they say.

No hope of an escape for them, no surfacing again, except in your dreams, in the breathing spaces between your dreams. Here they come, all the plungers you watched the water gulp and swallow, come specially to you, breathless to share discoveries, their buried treasure. Shells and bones, mate. Bygones. Be bygones.

Dice

A throw of loaded dice will abolish chance. But don't push your luck.

Treasure

How rich the language promises to make us, wealth come by hard or easy. We'll spend it like sailors ashore. It smells of blood, it tastes of metal, it weighs down the scales. Life-enhancing, life-destroying. Life-altering, surely.

This is the deep structure of that word-hoard, that glitter surface of thesaurus. Eight reales make one peso; pieces of eight, pure raucous silver. Clink. Eight escudos make one doubloon, golden as landfall dreams. Clink. Add sequins and moidres and pistoles and guineas for ballast, value calculable but incidence smaller. Clink. Therefore the sum (pieces of eight + doubloons + sequins + moidres + pistoles + guineas + assorted jewels + random silver and gold plate) = one dead man's chest, where x is his mark, where x is his status, where xbones rule, where x is the chromosome, where x marks the spot. Though a fistful of sand is a more usual outcome.

Parrot

Pirate. Parrot. Most letters in common. Some genes in common. Life expectancy: put your money on the parrot. Souls: keep your doubloons in your pocket.

Pirate. Parrot. A thing of shred and scratch, of excerpt and sample. Is there an echo here? Something at your shoulder, on your shoulder, tonight and every night in the cabaret of the shoulder, condensing lives to a few jaunty phrases, putting even yours in sardonic quotation marks. Speaking your life weight. Accounting for the dead, or those about to be. Pirate. Parrot. Pierrot. Pieces of eight.

Valerie R. Witte

from SILKYARD

[UNTIL THE TIME OF SPINNING]

3, AND THE MANY SHAPES OF CLAWS

[
To make
a strong
skeleton
two or
more reeling
the silk
borders
of fields
a form
in the sea
what
a mouth
wants
the ends
of limbs
]

[3.1]

To make a strong skeleton reestablish the laminar preventing

        a breakdown, originally | *She was starting to disappear*
                  herself | when applied

to the face subduing anatomy | *Under cloth or a woolen*
band, sunhats | then

           a crest between nipple and lip, suspended

a mesh of protein constructing small arteries | *If held*
back, of fullness

       pretended | fossils are expressions of locomotion, flagella

or wings, where contraction an elaborate network of appendages

        reduced to backbones | *And she hated the draft against her*
              scalp, a reminder | little

ropes hold eyes, set close | *To cover an absence, what shamed her* |

Receptors that register rigid | embedded the head is round

         with a mouth | *And she became practiced at avoiding*

flashes | leaves a caterpillar devouring a slight

      hump an inoffensive spine, especially flesh and connective

tissues such as tendon, ligament abundant

      in the gut, intervertebral | Was this *really a disease* | gelatin
                                       irreversibly

hydrolyzed | *Or an underlying condition of which she was partly*

      conscious | in the shape of a quarter-moon alongside five

pairs of false legs shed periodically, whole | *She knew naked*

   skin as a liability | the prismatic structure, mulberry | *The apparent*

futility of countering heredity | or lobed separately female and male,
pendulous

               catkins grown in rows |

Scott Thurston

Two Poems from *Moving*

late spring in the leafy autumn
merlin emerges from yew tree
screen ascending again –
potentiality only human if withheld
from the actual

to solve a cipher look out of the
window; particularity as the enemy of
the reading commons or this
intentionality somehow bound up
in a single self

between a show of public pain and the
divided closet upper partials added
to the chord, the implied basic line
slate paper weight to re-humanise
the picture of the work

unhampered by ulterior interest
the judgement of the siblings a
recognition of their resistance, burning
an effigy of the daemon to prevent
a return, repair the space

the dance making the rest of you
visible finding the wild line lost
the crowd placed a book
before me fear of locking in more
forcibly your snake dance

§

the knowledge that you need lives
in distinctions not reachable in the medium.
how do we begin? between that which is
about to happen and that which has and will
happen. fight for community's moments on the

ground of decisions taken in the present. how
a challenge challenges scale. you are not
alone again, nor willing to grant what you
can give because I want it too much.
movement is sacred where you reach the

limit of your habit. it has already started,
walking through the chartered feet inside
the mouth, away from and back to the
materials. stand close to a flat surface of
chance, local alignments, not successive instants.

in proximity to the nagging care in the
shop of lost objects an impending
ending to the dance in the upper room
to bring movement into consciousness against
the scepticism that cannot ever become

action. betrayed, discovered by movement.
turning up a new pathway in secure curious
acceptance, losing scale, making an issue of loose
leaf forms at ease in the intensity. coming back
from the dead, you have a right to be here.

juli Jana

ebb tide

gulls and waders wait
on rotting racks
              beneath wave-wash

lugworms hide
              burrow break
segments a-mix
              with shell & bone   stone
                                    & broken glass

whose eyes are those fixed vacantly
              like sea-sway scurrying
                       on sticks sideways

a head hardened flat
a mouth askew
hair entangled

                       amid the wet & waste
                       a fluorescent cold fire
              it cannot sink
              it cannot swim
can only
chase what drifts
in the wake
of breakers

the mercalli scale for measuring earthquakes

movement detected by instruments
felt by people resting

hanging lights sway
windows rattle
parked cars rock

small objects move
doors swing

trees sway
difficult to stand
objects fall off shelves
window glass shatters

hard to steer a car
bricks & tiles fall

people cling to trees
chimneys crack
tree branches snap
ground cracks

chimneys fall
underground pipes burst

rivers flood
buildings collapse
bridges destroyed
large gaps in ground

destruction

Kent MacCarter

The Plumbing Network under Dolores Park, San Francisco

after Thom Gunn

Off in to outer space you go my friends, I wish you bon voyage
  —Buffy Sainte-Marie, 'Moonshot'

1.
Outbid curiosity
download it
tonight. Beat it with grace
Make it squat. The long draw
of pig iron tells off its concrete. A big kid with chalk
sweating out murals
of hazard. Compact cars. Aprons of chug
it cups anthracite wax. Think
of all those boots
stamping in *Gunga Din*. Think of a bellydancer attempting to headstand
the baud rate of modems
swarming her legs
as Theremin antennae. Subterranean
frescoes pitching Campari
dries. Spawn. And with them, answers

2.
It knows a someone
who was never let to sort with dolls
when he was puny
                    so he bag-snatches from girls their security
front lawns or
heads on Halloween
peg leg and arms
leaving its demographic with half-filled carparks
metering atop *their* breastplate

93

3.
The ozone of the true. This is
what it deigns
to sniff. How it's wizened
by parking
a scooter so red only salmon will follow it next
to an off-Broadway disaster of vents
the Xerox headquarters requires
to digest. Their staff
is completely July with friends
Sumatra blend and mixed legumes
cramming for exams. It's teenage
a riot. Above the US Navy's corn chip aircraft
sonic boom and blow its toenails back to
9.30am. A low punch of meat
displaying the proper ticket in an all-day zone

4.
Painted Ladies
strut a plank
dropping straight
into Earth. Their aluminium gowns
and cheery wainscoting
parachute
down here they melt and recycle to black
pools, coal so
                    postmodern
bitcoins go variegated and tickle the pinkie
toe plugins
                    Above a female Clorox employee
begins to install
a recent browser
release, exploring for bridesmaids'
dresses to encase   all architectures
its tentacle code
brushing deep in limestone gossip

worming under the carpets and plummeting down
conduits
an overcommitted jellyfish
to hide-and-go-seek. She finds
an ideal cut on niemanmarcus.com
yet is stung by the price
                    Bullseye fresh
The oubliette itself.

5.
Things are getting altogether Beverly
around here
events of disposable razors. It. It cannot
plumb me
to swallow down
such blunted dazzle. It knows the Chippewa in Minnesota
got their man
Angelfood cake. And bait. On shoddy hustings a man
so primordial
he can dial up San Francisco Bay
a man without no
telephone. Sweet Jacalyn
obeys a corner.   Chews
her IP
address and believes no husband
of hers
shall hush-puppy with dolls. Or cry in basements
of a car wash
one below the next. Think of all those heels
in *Cabaret*. What would Isherwood make
say? And in what Pantone? What
is it?

Ulrike Almut Sandig

translated by Karen Leeder

ladies and gentlemen, if you please, listen
a hair's breadth to the side and beyond follow

the sound trace of the electronic poem on its path
past the speaker boxes. can you already see

music and sounds? can you already hear
the coloured lights? **the electronic poem**

is a poem within a poem and well
hidden in the wave forms of the future

that one moment later is already
our history. it hovers at the ears of Edgar

Varèse's grandchildren – and is past.

*after Edgard Varèse's **Poème électronique***

a little   group of
researchers from   Lauscha and Aachen
stubbornly claims that once there was something that looked
like a great and impossibly beautiful, a singing house with two
different-sized horns instead of a roof and, spanning from gable
to gable, its many wafer-thin walls, like otherwise only circus
tents have. oh absolute amateurs! those researchers from
Lauscha and Aachen are laughed out of court. but we still
believe them and scour their scribble for what is known of this
house: that is when you stroked it the doors would creak softly.
that when you went in, its three-hundred windows would begin
to hum. and when you wandered inside, moving pictures would
light up on the dark of the walls and you could scarcely believe
your own eyes. that's what was said in all the reports. post
scriptum it should be observed, the researchers from Lauscha
and Aachen called it a house. on this point, however, they were
mistaken. in reality it was the **poem of a house.**

after Edgard Varèse's **Poème électronique**

97

when the performance is over, the applause has died down, when the very last image of the woman and the child in her arms, can no longer be seen in the darkened hall, when the audience has gone back home and has had its own children, has brought them up and is grown imperceptibly small, smaller, and at last disappears, when even the hall has not stood there for years and only the blueprints and a handful of yellowing pictures are there to prove how uniquely beautiful it all was, and that inside it looked like the belly of a gigantic creature and that's how it sounded too – and after all that has gone, there's still this old **rumour**, that once there was something that looked like a great and impossibly beautiful, a singing house with two different-sized horns instead of a roof and, spanning

from gable to gable, its   many wafer-thin walls

like otherwise   only circus tents

after Edgard Varèse's **Poème électronique**

María do Cebreiro

translated by Neil Anderson

The Original

My red pencil follows the snow.
As it stepped it set new words free.

Before you they mumbled
inward.

After us they spoke.

The crows also did important work.

"Dark is my kingdom when you walk."

I throw the crown to the floor,
we share the time it takes
to get to my pencil:
"follow me, don't follow me."

And time, time burns up.
It burns and leaves no ash.

Our wine is acid but it's ours.

The Trace

I lost this poem.

You've also got to take into account
the crows' work.

It started out like this:

My red pencil.
Snow underlined.
Semen inside.

It ended like this:

Follow me, don't follow me.

Our wine is acid
but it's ours.

(Follow me, don't follow me.)

Loyalty

I tied up the manuscript. Smothered the words.
He said: "Untie me."

Do you want me to touch you like this?
I read his lips:
"Care for me. Don't cover me up."

You have my word.

The poems slipped from their bindings.

They create blood ties.
They work toward milk.

Earth

Inside it's really different. "Different from what?" More silent. "And what's it like being here?" There are no words. "Is that a compliment or an exaggeration?" You don't have to be cruel. "Words are my only defence." They don't protect you. You're too sweet. "Don't say anything." Do you mind if I smoke? "If we were outside I'd ask you to throw it on the ground." To crush it? "To watch the sparks fly when it hit the stones." Do you get lost too? "I get empty." Do you love me? "When he was little my brother used to eat dirt." Did he tell you what it tasted like? "I thought his mouth could be my home."

Field

(The sound of the water didn't keep her from seeing,
but rather from thinking.)

There were five of us: my friend, the kids,
the woman. There was someone else.
They left us behind.

—You almost never give names.

—The current shifted.
On the wooden bridge,
very quietly,
the third one said:
"Come with me. Don't be scared.
Hold on to my arm."

—Were you scared of the bridge or his arm?

—His insistence,
whispered, hard
as wood.

—What was his name?
—The bridge twisted round.

The woman, on the other side,
suggested
that I hike up
the hem of my dress.

"I've already been here." He doesn't believe her.

As splashes on the ground, the detergent
paints the sea on the stones.

—You use white paper. You don't recycle.

I think you are only capable of desire.

She's not offended. She smiles.

—You're not going to tell me I'm right?
—You don't need me to.

As she entered the river, the sound of the water blinded her.

—Were you compatible, the two of you?

—One day he asked me,
"do you sort your garbage?"

—Did you stop loving him?

—I came to understand
that sometimes he preferred
to suspect.

—He was probably scared.

—He wrote with his left hand.
She was far away.

We kept walking for a bit, I had said goodbye,
but he hadn't.

We lay down in the grass.

—One wouldn't think that you were
so sensitive to landscape.
—You know how I like
to improvise.
—Tickling, taking your clothes off,
turning away from the world.
—Changing my mind, rolling around,
playing. —Getting wet, seeing you
all together.
The river came later. Running clear.

It was one of those moments when it seems that things
give us continuity, that any old thing can
carry us on.

Very slowly, daylight crept
into the room. They breathe deeply.
Saying nothing, thinking nothing,
not even the air separates us.

The Code

When you go to enter, after the last number
what point will there be in knowing the code?

Everything you want to see is in the dark room.
You won't be able to see it for the dark.

That's my secret: your blindness.
That's your advantage: that I watch you.

We are the code. We have no key.

Notes on Contributors

NEIL ANDERSON is currently Visiting Assistant Professor of Spanish at Texas Tech University in Lubbock, Texas, and has a Ph.D. in Galician literature from the University of North Carolina, Chapel Hill.

ISOBEL ARMSTRONG has appeared Shearsman on several occasions. Her poetry features in the women's poetry anthology *Infinite Difference* (ed. Carrie Etter, Shearsman Books, 2010). Professor Emeritus of Birkbeck, University of London, her academic speciality is Victorian literature, and her publications include *Victorian Poetry: Poetry, Poetics and Politics* (1996) and *Victorian Glassworlds. Glass Culture and the Imagination* (2008).

PAULA BOHINCE lives in Pennsylvania and is the author of two collections from Sarabande: *Edge of Bayonet Woods* (2008) and *The Children* (2012).

PETER BOYLE lives in Sydney. His most recent collection is a new and selected poems, *Towns in the Great Desert*, from Puncher & Wattman. His translation of José Kozer's *Tokonoma* is due from Shearsman in October 2014.

MARÍA DO CEBREIRO is a Galician poet, whose collection *I am not from here* was published by Shearsman in translation by Helena Miguélez-Carballeira in 2010. Her Galician collections include *Nos, as inadaptas* (2002) and *Os hemisferios* (2006).

M.T.C. CRONIN lives in Queensland. An award-winning Australian poet, she has two collections from Shearsman (with a third, *in possession of loss*, coming in late 2014) as well as a volume co-authored with Peter Boyle.

ANAMARÍA CROWE SERRANO lives in Dublin. Her first poetry collection, *Femispheres,* was published by Shearsman Books in 2008. A translator from Spanish and Italian, she also edits the online journal, *Colony*.

RAY DIPALMA lives in New York City. His many publications include *The Ancient Use of Stone: Journals and Daybooks 1998-2008* (Otis Books / Seismicity Editions, 2009).

TIM DOOLEY lives in London, and is Head of English and Film Studies at Rickmansworth School, Herts. His first collection *The Interrupted Dream* was published by Anvil in 1985. His most recent publications are both from Salt: *Keeping Time* (2009) and *Imagined Rooms* (2010).

MICHAEL FARRELL lives in Melbourne; his most recent collection, *Open Sesame*, was published in Sydney by Giramondo in 2012. He recently won *Australian Book Review*'s Peter Porter Poetry Prize.

DAMIAN FURNISS lives in Exeter. His first collection, *Chocolate Che*, was published by Shearsman in 2009. The poems in this issue will appear in his next collection, *The Best of All Possible Worlds* (Shearsman 2015).

MARK GOODWIN received a substantial Grant for the Arts from Arts Council England in 2013, to develop sound-enhanced poetry. A sound-enhanced version of *Something Slips Through Lock Gates at Foxton* can be heard on Mark's SoundCloud site: soundcloud.com/kramawoodgin. In April 2014, Mark and Longbarrow Press put on an international exhibition of sound-enhanced poetry focusing on place and landscape, installed in Leicester's Cube Gallery (at The Phoenix), and called *Poems, Places & Soundscapes*. The contents of this exhibition can now be explored online at poemsplacessoundscapes.wordpress.com

ANNE GORRICK lives in upper New York State. She has three Shearsman collections: *Kyotologic* (2008), *I-Formation Book 1* (2011) and *Book 2* (2012).

JEREMY HOOKER has published two volumes of his journals with Shearsman, most recently *Openings — A European Journal* (2014). His Collected Poems, *The Cut of the Light* was published by Enitharmon in 2006.

JULI JANA is a London-based artist and poet, whose chapbook *ra-t* was published by Shearsman in June 2014.

NORMAN JOPE has published several books, including *Dreams of the Caucasus* (Shearsman), *The Book of Bells and Candles* and *Aphinar* (Waterloo Press).

KAREN LEEDER's translations of German poetry have appeared in a variety of journals including *Poetry Review, PN Review, Domus* (Italy), *SPORT* (New Zealand) and *MPT*. Her volume of Evelyn Schlag's *Selected Poems* with Carcanet in 2004 won the Schlegel Tieck Prize in 2005 and her translations of Durs Grünbein won *The Times* Stephen Spender Prize in 2013. She received a Deutsche Übersetzerfonds award for her translation of Ulrike Almut Sandig in 2014 and will translate Sandig's *Flamingos* for Liverpool University Press.

KENT MACCARTER is Managing Editor of *Cordite Poetry Review* in Australia. He lives in Castlemaine and is the author of three collections— *In the Hungry Middle of Here* (Transit Lounge, 2009), *Ribosome Spreadsheet* (Picaro, 2011) and *Sputnik's Cousin* (Transit Lounge, 2014). He is also editor of *Joyful Strains: Making Australia Home* (Affirm Press, 2013), a non-fiction collection of diasporic memoir.

JULIE MACLEAN, born in Bristol but now in Australia, is the author of *When I saw Jimi* (Indigo Dreams) and *Kiss of the Viking* (Poetry Salzburg). Shortlisted for The Crashaw Prize (Salt), her poetry and short fiction features in leading international journals and *The Best Australian Poetry* (UQP). Forthcoming in *Poetry*. Blogs at www.juliemacleanwriter.com

ALASDAIR PATERSON lives in Exeter. His latest Shearsman collection is *elsewhere or thereabouts* (2014).

PETER ROBINSON is a professor at Reading University and has two collections with Shearsman, plus several edited volumes — most recently, Roy Fisher's 'Occasional Prose', *An Easily Bewildered Child* — a book of aphorisms and another of interviews. His next collection, *Buried Music*, will appear from Shearsman in January 2015.

ULRIKE ALMUT SANDIG was born in 1979 in Großenhain, Saxony, in 1979 and now lives in Berlin. In 2001, together with the songwriter Marlen Pelny, she founded the literature performance projects 'augenpost' (eyemail) and 'ohrenpost' (earmail). In 2005 she completed a degree in Theology and Modern Indology and in 2010 she graduated from the German Literary Institute in Leipzig. She has published three collections of poetry: *Zunder* (2005/2009); *Streumen* (2007) and *Dickicht* (2011), as well as short stories and radio plays. She has been granted residencies in Helsinki and Sydney and won numerous prizes, including the prestigious Leonce-und-Lena Prize (2009) and, most recently, the Droste Emerging Talent Award (2012).

LUCY SHEERMAN lives in Cambridge. She is the author of *Rarefied (falling without landing)* from Oystercatcher Press, and also appeared in the Shearsman anthology, *Infinite Difference*, in 2010.

NATHAN SHEPHERDSON lives in the Glass House Mountains in Queensland. His first book, *Sweeping the Light Back into the Mirror* (UQP 2006), won the Mary Gilmore Award in 2008. In 2008 also he released *what marian drew never told me about light* (Small Change Press) and in 2009 *Apples with Human Skin* was published by University of Queensland Press. In 2013 he published his fifth collection, *the day the artists stood still (vol. 1)* (Another Lost Shark, Brisbane).

SCOTT THURSTON lives in Manchester, where he teaches at Salford University. The most recent of his three Shearsman collections is *Internal Rhyme* (2011).

CRISTINA VITI is a widely-published poet and translator. Her translation of Mariapia Veladiano's award-winning novel *A Life Apart* was published by MacLehose Press in 2013, and a new version of Dino Campana's *Orphic Songs* is forthcoming from Waterloo Press. Her translations of the Albanian poet Gëzim Hajdari will appear from Shearsman in 2015.

HEIDI WILLIAMSON, who lives in Norwich, makes her first appearance in the magazine in this issue. Her first collection, *Electric Shadow*, was published by Bloodaxe in 2011. She was poet-in-residence for the London Science Museum's Dana Centre in 2008 and 2009, and is currently poet-in-residence at the John Jarrold Printing Museum.

VALERIE R. WITTE makes her debut in *Shearsman* with this issue. She is a member of Kelsey Street Press, which publishes experimental writing by women, and is a co-founder of the Bay Area Correspondence School, which aims to explore the impact of digital culture on contemporary writers. Her chapbook, *The History of Mining*, was published by the g.e. collective, and her manuscript, *A Game of Correspondence*, was a finalist for the 2013 Gatewood Prize (Switchback Books).

New Titles from Shearsman Books

José Kozer: *Tokonoma* (translated by Peter Boyle) — Bilingual edition, £14.95
José Kozer: *Tokonoma* (translated by Peter Boyle) — English edition, £9.95
Alberto Arvelo Torrealba: *Florentino and The Devil*
(translated by Timothy Adès), £9.95
Pablo de Rokha: *Selected Poems* (translated by Urayoán Noël), £12.95
Trevor Joyce: *Selected Poems 1967-2014*, £9.95
Niamh O'Mahony (ed.) *Essays on the Poetry of Trevor Joyce*, £14.95

Lightning Source UK Ltd.
Milton Keynes UK
UKOW03f0706130914

238478UK00002B/40/P

9 781848 613833